IMAGES OF WAR
FINAL DAYS OF THE REICH

IMAGES OF WAR
FINAL DAYS OF THE REICH

IAN BAXTER

Pen & Sword
MILITARY

First published in Great Britain in 2011 by
PEN & SWORD MILITARY
an imprint of
Pen & Sword Books Ltd,
47 Church Street, Barnsley,
South Yorkshire.
S70 2AS

Copyright © Ian Baxter 2011

ISBN 978-1-84884-381-3

A CIP catalogue record for this book is available
from the British Library

Typeset by Mac Style, Beverley, East Yorkshire
Printed and bound in Great Britain by CPI

Pen & Sword Books Ltd incorporates the imprints of
Pen & Sword Books Ltd incorporates the Imprints of Pen & Sword Aviation,
Pen & Sword Family History, Pen & Sword Maritime, Pen & Sword Military, Pen & Sword
Discovery, Wharncliffe Local History, Wharncliffe True Crime, Wharncliffe Transport,
Pen & Sword Select, Pen & Sword Military Classics, Leo Cooper, The Praetorian Press,
Remember When, Seaforth Publishing and Frontline Publishing

For a complete list of Pen & Sword titles please contact:
PEN & SWORD BOOKS LIMITED
47 Church Street, Barnsley, South Yorkshire, S70 2AS, England.
E-mail: enquiries@pen-and-sword.co.uk
Website: www.pen-and-sword.co.uk

Contents

Introduction

Drawing on a superb collection of rare German photographs this new Images of War series covers the last battles fought by the Wehrmacht and their SS counterparts following their crushing defeat on the Eastern Front. These German forces that survived the constant enemy artillery barrages, the onslaught of the tank armadas and mass infantry assaults, had streamed back westwards, towards the river Oder, the last bastion of defence before Berlin, where they continued fighting vicious defensive battles until there units either run out of ammunition or were killed.

Throughout the book it provides an absorbing insight into the bitter final days of the Reich. It reveals how the remnants of Hitler's once vaunted force were hurled back into a devastated Reich and ordered to wage an unprecedented war of attrition against an overwhelming foe. Along the River Oder where the German soldier stood on the fringes of the Reich capital they were ordered to fight a series of colossal blood-thirsty battles in a desperate attempt to hold the disintegrating front. It reveals in detail, accompanied by extensive in-depth captions, how the Germans were slowly driven from their decimated positions and forced to fight, being pushed further west until they stood fighting in the rubble strewn streets of Berlin. But Hitler still obsessed with the belief that fanatical aggression could hold-back the enemy tried to pour the last of his resources into the battle in a fanatical attempt to win time.

The Final Days of the Reich is a unique study of a struggling German Army trying in vain to avoid being sucked into a maelstrom of destruction. From the last battles fought on Russian and Baltic soil, to the final show-down in front of Berlin, the book reveals an horrendous story of an armies desperate attempt to survive in one of the most important visual records of Germany's demise of the Reich.

Photographic Acknowledgements

It is with the greatest pleasure that I use this opportunity on concluding this book to thank those who helped make this volume possible. My expressions of gratitude first goes to my photographic collector Michael Cremin. He has been an unfailing source; supplying me with a number of photographs that were obtained from numerous private sources.

In Poland I am also extremely grateful to Marcin Kaludow, my Polish photographic specialist, who supplied me with a variety of photographs that he sought from private photographic collections in Poland.

Chapter 1

Defending the East

During the last months of 1944 the situation for the German soldier on the Eastern Front was dire. They had fought desperately to maintain cohesion and hold their meagre positions that often saw thousands perish. By September 1944 they were still holding a battle line more than 1,400 miles in overall length, which had been severely weakened by the overwhelming strength of the Red Army. To make matters worse troop units were no longer being refitted with replacements to compensate for the large losses sustained. Supplies of equipment and ammunition too were so insufficient in some areas of the front that commanders were compelled to ration ammunition to their men. As a consequence many soldiers had become increasingly aware that they were in the final stages of the war in the East, and this included battle-hardened combatants. They had also realized that they were now fighting an enemy that was far superior to them. As a consequence in a number of sectors of the front soldiers were able to realistically assess the war situation and this in turn managed to save the lives of many that would normally have been killed fighting to the last man.

In spite of the adverse situation in which the German soldier was placed he was still strong and determined to fight with courage and skill. During the last six months of the war the German soldier had expended considerable combat efforts lacking sufficient reconnaissance and the necessary support of tanks and heavy weapons to ensure any type of success. Ultimately, the German soldier during the last months of the war was ill prepared against any type of large-scale offensive. The infantry defensive positions relied upon sufficient infantry ammunition supply and the necessary support to ensure that they would able to hold their fortified areas. Without this, the German soldier was doomed. Commanders in the field were fully aware of the significant problems and the difficulties imposed by committing badly equipped soldiers to defend the depleted lines of defence. However, in the end, they had no other choice than to order their troops to fight with whatever they had at their disposal.

In the last months of the war German forces continued retreating across a scarred and devastated wasteland. On both the Western and Eastern Fronts, the last agonising moments of the war were played out. Whilst the British and American troops were poised to cross the River Rhine, in the East the terrifying advance of the Red Army was bearing down on the River Oder, pushing back the last remnants of Hitler's exhausted units.

Due to a serious lack of troop reserves many parts of the front were now defended by a mixed number of local militia, postal defence units, locally raised anti-tank groups, *Wehrmacht*, *Waffen-SS* and *Allegemeine-SS* formations, *Hitlerjugend*, and units of the *Volkssturm*. But surprisingly, even in the rank and file of the *Volkssturm*, morale remained high. For these ordinary men of Germany's Home Guard units they needed no propaganda to urge them on. They knew, like all those defending the Fatherland that they were fighting now to defend their homes and loved ones. All that what was left to them was their skill and courage. Everything else, guns, planes, and armoured vehicles had already been sacrificed. Spread among these under-armed forces was a mixed bag of strong and weak *Wehrmacht* and *Waffen-SS* troops. In some areas of the front there were good defensive lines comprising mazes of intricate blockhouses and trenches. Towns that fell in the path of these defensive belts were evacuated. Thousands of women, children and old men were removed from their dwellings and some were actually pressed into service to help construct massive anti-tank ditches and other obstacles.

A typical strongpoint deployed along the front during the last weeks of 1944 contained MG 34 and MG 42 machine guns on light and heavy mountings, anti-tank rifle company or battalion, a sapper platoon that was equipped with a host of various explosives, infantry guns, anti-tank artillery company which had a number of anti-tank guns, and occasionally a self-propelled gun.

Operating at intervals were Pz.Kpfw.IVs, Tigers, Panthers tanks, and a number of StuG.III assault guns, all of which were scraped together. This front-line defensive belt was designated as a killing zone where every possible anti-tank weapon and artillery piece would be used to ambush Soviet tanks. Whilst an enemy tank was subjected to a storm of fire within the kill zone, special engineer mobile detachments equipped with anti-personnel and anti-tank mines would quickly deploy and erect new obstacles, just in case other tanks managed to escape the zone.

If the crew from a disabled tank had survived the initial attack and bailed out, special sapper units were ordered to pick off the unwary. However, whilst it appeared that the Germans were prepared for a Soviet attack, much of the equipment employed along the defensive belts was too thinly spread. Commanders too were unable to predict exactly where the strategic focal point of the Soviet attack would take place. To make matters worse when the Russians begun heavily bombing German positions all along the frontier, this also severely weakened the strongest defensive lines.

Along the frontier of the Reich the German defensive lines were soon turned into a wall of flame and smoke as the Russians launched their attacks. For the *Volkssturm* and *Hitlerjugend*, many were going into action for the first time, and a number of them felt excited at the thought of fighting an offensive that their *Führer* had said would drive the invaders from their homeland and win new victories in the East. But this conflict was without rule, and new conscripts soon learned the terrors of fighting superior Russian soldiers. Under-armed and under-trained, these soldiers were quickly driven from their meagre defensive positions and pulverized into the rubble. When some determined units refused to budge, the Russians ordered in their flame-throwers to burn them out. Any *Volkssturm* men that were found among captured prisoners were normally regarded as partisans and simply herded together like cattle and executed. In some cases, Russian tanks deliberately ran over the wounded, or hanged them from surrounding trees or lamp posts.

Elsewhere along the frontier of the Reich the Red Army drive gathered momentum with more towns and villages falling to the onrushing forces. Suicidal opposition from a few *SS* and *Wehrmacht* strong points bypassed in earlier attacks reduced buildings to a blasted rubble. Everywhere it seemed the Germans were being constantly forced to retreat. Many isolated units spent hours or even days fighting a bloody defence. Russian soldiers frequently requested them to surrender and assured them that no harm would come to them if they did so. But despite this reassuring tone, most German troops continued to fight to the end.

A stationary Sd.Kfz.10 halftrack in the snow mounting a 2cm FlaK. These deadly guns were much respected by low-flying Russian airmen and were also particularly devastating against light vehicles, as well as troops caught in the open. The weapon also armed a variety of vehicles on self-propelled mounts where they could be moved from one part of the defensive line to another quickly and efficiently.

A soldier with a range finder is calculating the distance and location of enemy aircraft so that his FlaK gun battery can range in on its position and fire with more accuracy. Note how his white winter camouflage garment has been soiled with dirt following constant use.

Three photographs showing grenadiers hitching a lift on board StuG III, Ausf. G and StuH assault guns during winter defensive operations in 1944. Panzergrenadiers were considered elite frontline units and were known for their frontline mobility. Often they would advance into battle with assault guns and other armoured vehicles, which offered them armour protection and mobility until they were close enough to attack enemy positions on foot.

An interesting photograph showing a halted Sd.Kfz.251/9 Ausf.C in the snow. The crew are visibly trying to deduce the whereabouts of their enemy through field binoculars. When the Pz.Kpfw.IV was up-armed with the 7.5cm KwK 40 L/43, the short 7.5cm KwK 37 L/24 gun barrel became redundant. However, it was soon decided that these short barrelled guns be converted and mounted on a number of halftracks, notably the 9 series of the Sd.Kfz.251. These vehicles did sterling service in the East, but like so many new improved weapons in the German arsenal the few employed for combat made little difference to the outcome of a battle.

A commanding officer inside an Sd.Kfz.251 halftrack during defensive operations in Poland in early 1945. The officer is wearing the distinctive winter reversible jacket white-side out. The principal objective of the Red Army was to crush the remaining German forces in Poland, East Prussia and the Baltic states. Along the Baltic an all-out Russian assault had begun in earnest with the sole intention of crushing the remaining understrength German units that had once formed Army Group North.

A column of vehicles including one or perhaps two Sd.Kfz.251 halftracks, numerous Wespe 10.5cm SP howitzers and, just below the crest of the road, a Pz.Kfw.IV advancing along a road in the depth of the winter in late 1944. The Panzerwaffe continued to rigidly commit everything it still had. Despite the dogged resistance of many of the tank crews and supporting troops, there was no coherent strategy, and any local counter-offensives were often blunted with severe losses. The Soviets possessed too many tanks, anti-tank guns and aircraft for the Panzers and they remained incapable of causing any serious losses or delay.

A Panzergrenadier protects himself from enemy fire by hiding himself at the rear of a destroyed Pz.Kpfw.IV. Note the captured Russian PPSh-41 submachine gun. This submachine gun, nicknamed by the Russians as the 'Finka', was widely used by the German Army throughout the war, and in larger quantities during the last months. It was rugged, reliable, and had a large magazine capacity.

Three Wehrmacht troops converse standing next to a whitewashed halftrack during a lull in defensive operations in Poland in January 1945. For many there was a gloomy conviction that the war was lost. Being always outnumbered, perpetually short of fuel and ammunition, and having to constantly exert themselves and their machinery to the very limits of endurance it all had a profound effect on life at the front.

Waffen-SS troops inside a forest during the Red Army offensive in January 1945. During the last months of the war the SS did receive a high proportion of tanks, artillery and assault guns, but this was in stark contrast to the enormous volume of armaments being produced by the Russians. The SS were thus faced with a dangerous and worsening prospect, but unlike the normal German soldier many of these elite troops retained their fanatical determination on the battlefield.

Two photographs showing mortar crews during operations on the Eastern Front. They are equipped with the 8cm sGrW 34 mortar. Each battalion fielded some six of these excellent 8cm sGrW 34 mortars, which could fire 15 projectiles per minute to a range of 2,625 yards. Aside from high-explosive and smoke bombs, this weapon also fired a 'bouncing' bomb. It was very common for infantry, especially during intensive long periods of action, to fire their mortar from either trenches or dug-in positions where the mortar crew could also be protected from enemy fire.

Two PaK gunners stand next to their obsolete 7.5cm PaK 97/38, a French weapon used by the Germans in the early stages of Barbarossa. In many areas in Poland and along the borders of the Reich German units fought with distinction to contain the Russians from breaking through. However, the unrelenting fighting had proven to be more costly. As the winter of 1944–45 progressed a feeling of further despair and gloom prevailed across the entire German Army. To the depressed soldiers that had to endure the fourth Russia winter a gloomy conviction gripped them that soon they would be defending their own villages and towns against the onrushing Red Army.

A Panzergrenadier dressed in his winter whites is armed with the deadly Panzerfaust and the StG 44 (*Sturmgewehr 44*) *assault rifle*. During the last year of the war the Panzerfaust was used extensively to combat Russian armour. It was a handheld rocket-propelled grenade, which was effective at a range of about 30 metres.

A photograph caught the moment a parked Panzerwerfer is launched into fire mission against an advancing enemy target. This version was designated as the Sd.Kfz.4/1 and consisted of an armoured Maultier body with a ten-shot 15 Nebelwerfer 42 rocket launcher mounted on the roof.

A Waffen-SS StuG crew have halted during the last stages of the defence of western Poland during the winter of 1944-45. Despite the StuG's proven tank-killing potential and its service on the battlefield, the vehicle gradually deprived both Wehrmacht and Waffen-SS infantry of the vital fire support for which the assault gun was originally built, in order to supplement the massive losses in the Panzerwaffe. By January 1945 conditions within the ranks of the Panzerwaffe were so bad that many vehicles were simply abandoned due to the lack of fuel or ammunition stocks.

Panzergrenadiers wearing their distinctive winter white camouflage smocks follow a late variant Pz.Kpfw.IV along an icy road. The vehicles side skirts are still intact. These skirts were constructed of mild steel plates and were very effective against close range enemy anti-tank rifles but not always effective against high explosive shells high explosive shells.

A Kleines Kettenkraftrad Sd.Kfz.2 halftrack moves along a typical eastern European road. These small motorcycle halftracks were widely used during the war on the Eastern Front, especially in the last two years of the campaign. They were very versatile machines and often hauled trailers and laid cable communications.

Two photographs showing a Waffen-SS 8.8cm FlaK crew with their white washed weapon during winter operations. By 1944, SS mechanized formations had become very well equipped with FlaK guns. A typical SS Panzer-Division during this period was authorized with 12 heavy 8.8cm FlaK pieces, while less well equipped SS grenadier and Gebirgsjäger divisions still only possessed one or two, or none at all.

15cm Nebelwerfer 41 can be seen with part of its deadly six-barreled rocket tubes hidden by foliage. This weapon fired 2.5kg shells that could be projected over a range of 7,000 metres. When fired the projectiles screamed through the air, causing the enemy to become unnerved by the noise. Because it was dangerous for the crew to remain close to the launcher while the piece was being fired, it was fired remotely using an electric switch and cable attached to the mortar.

A Waffen-SS soldier withdraws with his men through a deserted village either in Poland or the Baltic States in the winter of 1944–45. Slowly and tenaciously the SS soldier retreated back across a bleak and hostile landscape, always outnumbered, constantly low on fuel, ammunition and other desperate supplies. All this and the continuous pressure from their Führer to defend every yard of land with their blood, made fighting even more inhumane.

White washed Panther tanks operating somewhere on the Baltic front. Along the German Baltic front the Germans were experiencing defensive problems in many areas and despite strong fortified positions, which were manned with PaK guns and lines of machine gun pits, the Red Army moved forward in their hundreds regardless of the cost in life to their own ranks. All along the battered and blasted front German troops tried in vain to hold their positions against overwhelming odds. Whilst a number of areas simply cracked under the sheer weight of the Russian onslaught, there were numerous areas where German units continued to demonstrate their ability to defend the most hazardous positions against well-prepared and highly superior enemy forces.

A well dug-in mortar crew. By the end of 1944 German front line positions were badly strained, and the bulk of German forces no longer had sufficient supplies or manpower to maintain their positions for any appreciable length of time. German troops, battered and bruised from months of ceaseless combat, were desperately trying to hold position but the situation had deteriorated far quicker than the German High Command had anticipated.

Two photographs showing a FlaK position in the snow somewhere in Army Group North. The unrelenting attacks began to increasingly wear down the defenders, and Red Army continued to push the front back further west. The bulk of the German force was now short on food and ammunition, and relied mainly on draught animals to haul their guns from one battle front to another. All seemed lost, but amazingly, the weary and exhausted troops still held many of their positions.

A mortar crew in one of the many defensive positions that littered the Eastern Front. The Germans were suffering from an unmistakable lack of provisions. Many units were simply being thrown into battle as piecemeal, their commanders hoping that it would stem the enemies drive westward. To Hitler the defence of Poland and the Baltic States were the last bastion of defence in the East before the Reich was invaded. Every soldier, he said, was to continue to 'stand and fight' and wage an unprecedented battle of attrition.

A variety of vehicles and weapons on tow during defensive operations in the Baltic States. The German soldier was fighting a foe with at least six-to-one numerical superiority. All along the front Russian aircraft and artillery bombarded the German lines, trying to reduce the front into small pockets of resistance. In many areas, however, the Germans were able to repel these attacks and even launched a series of attacks of their own aimed at blunting the Russian drive. Although the Germans suffered high casualties, Red Army losses were far worse.

Two photographs showing StuG.III's halted in the snow. All along the front lines the Germans became increasingly hard pressed to hold their lines. In some areas of the front as German forces began retreating westward they were steadily ground down in a battle of attrition and could no longer remain cohesive on the battlefield. The Russians in overwhelming superiority advanced across the flat plains of Poland and the Baltic States using both fields and the long straight highways. Panzergrenadiers, *Luftwaffe* field units, *Waffen-SS*, *Hitlerjungend* and *Volkssturm* conscripts tried in vain to hold back the enemy onslaught.

Chapter 2

Last Battles in the East

The last great offensive that brought the Russians their final victory in the East began during the third week of January 1945. The principal objective was to crush the remaining German forces in Poland, East Prussia and the Baltic states. Along the front an all-out Russian assault had begun in earnest with the sole intention of crushing the remaining understrength German units that had once formed *Heeresgruppe Nord*. It was these heavy, sustained attacks that eventually restricted the German-held territory in the north-east to a few small pockets of land surrounding four ports: Libau, Kurland, Pillau in East Prussia and Danzig at the mouth of the River Vistula.

Here along the Baltic coast the German defenders attempted to stall the massive Russian push with the remaining weapons and men they had at their disposal. Every German soldier defending the area was aware of the consequences of being captured. Not only would the coastal garrisons be cut off and eventually destroyed, but also masses of civilian refugees would be prevented from escaping from those ports by sea. Hitler made it quite clear that all remaining *Wehrmacht*, *Waffen-SS* volunteer units, and *Luftwaffe* personnel were not to evacuate, but to stand and fight and wage an unprecedented battle of attrition. In fact, what Hitler had done by a single sentence was to condemn to death 8,000 officers and more than 181,000 soldiers and *Luftwaffe* personnel.

In southwest Poland the strategic town of Breslau situated on the River Oder had been turned into a fortress and defended by various *Volkssturm*, *Hitlerjugend*, *Waffen-SS* and various formations from the 269.Infantry-Division. During mid-February 1945 the German units put up a staunch defence with every available weapon that they could muster. As the battle ensued, both German soldiers and civilians were cut to pieces by Russian attacks. During these viscous battles, which lasted until May 1945, there were many acts of courageous fighting. Cheering and yelling, old men and boys of the *Volkssturm* and *Hitlerjugend*, supported by ad hoc *SS* units, advanced across open terrain, sacrificing themselves in front of well-positioned Russian machine gunners and snipers. By the first week of March, Russian infantry had driven back the defenders into the inner city and were pulverising it street by street. Lightly clad *SS*, *Volkssturm* and *Hitlerjugend* were still seen resisting, forced to fight in the sewers beneath the decimated city. When Breslau finally capitulated almost 60,000 Russian soldiers were killed or wounded trying to the capture the town, with some 29,000 German military and civilian casualties.

Elsewhere on the Eastern Front, fighting was merciless, with both sides imposing harsh measures on their men to stand where they were and fight to the death. With every defeat and withdrawal came ever-increasing pressure on the commanders to exert harsher discipline on their weary men. The thought of fighting on German soil for the first time resulted in mixed feelings among the soldiers. Although the defence of the *Reich* automatically stirred emotional feelings to fight for their land, not all soldiers felt the same way. More and more young conscripts were showing signs that they did not want to die for a lost cause. Conditions on the Eastern Front were miserable not only for the newest recruits, but also for battle-hardened soldiers who had survived many months of bitter conflict against the Red Army. The cold harsh weather during February and March prevented the soldiers digging trenches more than a metre down. But the main problems that confronted the German forces during this period were shortages of ammunition, fuel and vehicles. Some vehicles in a division could only be used in an emergency and battery fire was strictly prohibited without permission from the commanding officer. The daily ration on average per division was for two shells per gun.

As the great Red Army drive gathered momentum, more towns and villages fell to the onrushing forces. Suicidal opposition from a few *SS* and *Wehrmacht* strong points bypassed in earlier attacks reduced buildings to blasted rubble. Everywhere it seemed the Germans were being constantly forced to retreat. Many isolated units spent hours or even days fighting a bloody defence. Russian soldiers frequently requested them to surrender and assured them that no harm would come to them if they did so. But despite this reassuring tone, most German troops continued to fight to the bitter end. To the German soldier in 1945 they were fighting an enemy that they not only despised, but were also terrified of. Many soldiers, especially those fighting in the ranks of the *Waffen-SS* decided that would meet their fate out on the battlefield. To them they would rather bleed fighting on the grasslands of Eastern Europe than surrender and be at the mercy of a Russian soldier.

Along the Baltic States the German soldier too was totally aware of the significance if it were lost. They knew that their *Führer* was determined more than ever to drag out the war and help stave off a Russian drive on Berlin. For this reason he told his battlefront commanders to instil every soldier to fight to the death for every city, town and village. One such city he was fanatical in defending was the ancient Teutonic city of Danzig. Danzig was populated almost exclusively by Germans and before the war had been designated a free city giving Poland access to the Baltic Sea. This had angered Hitler bitterly and churned-up great bitterness and a determination to reclaim the city back. It was on this pretence that Hitler attacked Poland in 1939, and engulfed Europe into a World War. Now five years later he was determined not to let the city fall without a bloody fight.

For some weeks Danzig had been preparing itself for a long-drawn out defence. Fighting to the east of the city in early March 1945 was the *2.Armee*. For several days the *2.Armee* fought well against the full weight of the Second Belorussian Front. A number of German divisions put up a staunch defence notably from the 4.Panzer-Division. However, fighting was so fierce that the division was savagely mauled and pushed westwards with its remnants doggedly combating from one fixed position to another.

Inside the city Danzig was being defended by a mixture of infantry, *Panzertruppen*, *Volkssturm*, and *Hitlerjugend*. The main armoured force comprised of the 4.Panzer-Division which consisted of Panzer-Regiment 35, *Artillerie-Regiment 103*, and *Panzer Aufklaerungs Abteilung 4*, and two regiments of *Panzergrenadiere*. The first battalion of the Panzer-Regiment 35 was equipped with Panther tanks, while the second battalion was equipped with Pz.Kpfw IV's. The artillery regiment was equipped mainly with Wespe and Hummel self-propelled howitzers, and towed howitzers and guns.

Although the Germans were poorly matched in terms of equipment and supply a number of the troops were hardened veterans that had survived some of the most costly battles in the East. Hurriedly these troops were positioned along the main roads leading into the city.

Heavy machine gun platoons dug-in and held each end of the line while the remainder were scattered in various buildings. Armoured vehicles from Panzer-Regiment 35 took-up key positions in order to defend the main thoroughfare leading into the centre of the city, although not one single tank was battle ready. Crude obstacles were also erected, and troops were emplaced in defensive positions armed with a motley assortment of anti-tank and FlaK guns, machine guns, Panzerfaust and the deadly Panzerschrek.

When Russian tanks were identified entering the suburbs on 24 March, *Wehrmacht*, *Panzertruppen*, *Volkssturm*, and *Hitlerjugend* laden with guns and ammunition, suddenly sprang into action. Moving rapidly through the deserted streets Russian tanks pushed forward accompanied by infantry. In an instant the Germans opened-up a crescendo of fire. A number of Soviet tanks burst into flames before they could wrench open a route into the city. However, superior Soviet strength soon began overwhelming the suburbs. For hours it seemed each soldier was engaged in an individual contest of attrition. House to house fighting raged. Infiltrating the buildings Russians fought a series of deadly hand-to-hand battles with Germans using bayonets, knives and grenades. Anti-tank, machine gun and mortar fire were brought to bear on anything that moved. Germans commanders were all too aware of the significant strength of their resilient foe and hoped that they could contain the Red Army for as long as possible. The Russians mercilessly tore through the suburbs of the city and lay to waste every building in its path. A mixture of armoured vehicles mainly from Panzer-Regiment 35, tried to contain parts of the city from becoming overrun. The attack through the city was swift, but from every conceivable point, German troops poured a lethal storm of fire onto the advancing troops.

By 26 March the whole city had been engulfed in a sea of smoke and flame. German troops became more aggressive as the urban battle intensified. Slowly and methodically the Russians began taking one district after another, pushing back the defenders in a storm of fire and heavy infantry assaults. Whole areas were totally obliterated by tanks and artillery. Many Germans that were captured or wounded were executed on the spot and left suspended from the lamp posts as a warning to others. In parts of the city *Volkssturm* and Hitlerjugend support by a mixture of *Wehrmacht* and Panzer troops, managed to knock out a number of Russian tanks with Panzerfaust and Panzerschreck. But even these courageous fighters were no match for hardened soldiers that had fought their way bitterly through Russia to the gates of the Reich. German commanders tried their best to instil hope and determination in the poorly armed defenders, but district after district still fell to the Russian advance.

By 29 March those that had not been encircled or annihilated inside the city fled to mouth of the Vistula. Although the following day Danzig fell, resistance was not totally suppressed. A number of defiant groups that had been encircled and refused to capitulate fought on until they were annihilated.

Elsewhere along the Baltic coast and further south on the German central front the situation for the German Army was spiralling out of control, in spite fanatical resistance. German commanders in the field now resigned themselves with the gloomy prospect of not being able of hold back the Red Army for any appreciable length of time, and the news sent shock waves through the German High Command. For them it marked the beginning of the Soviet invasion of the Fatherland. As German forces fought to delay the inevitable capture of East Prussia, the main bulk of the Red Army drive bypassed various pockets of resistance and spilled out into eastern Pomerania and the Prussian province of Pomerania, where it fought a number of hard-pressed battles.

A StuG.III Ausf. G crew pose for the camera inside a snow covered forest. By January 1945 the equipment situation had deteriorated greatly, especially in the armoured units. The condition of German formations was a constant concern for the tacticians. Even in January and February 1945 they still did receive some tanks, artillery and assault guns, but this was in stark contrast to the enormous volume of armaments being produced by the Russians. The Germans were thus faced with a dangerous and worsening prospect of soon being defeated on home soil.

Troops marching along a frozen road. All along the battered and blasted front German troops tried in vain to hold their positions against overwhelming odds. Whilst a number of areas simply cracked under the sheer weight of the Russian onslaught, there were many places where German units continued to demonstrate their ability to defend the most hazardous positions against well-prepared and greatly superior enemy forces.

The crew of a 10.5cm FH 18 rest during a lull in the fighting. The sheer power of this weapon could hurl its destructive charge up to 10,675m (11,675yds) away. By 1943 only a few of these guns remained in active service and were used mainly in Russia until the end of the war.

A photograph showing a 10.5cm FH 18 heavy field howitzer being readied for action beside a building. The 10.5cm field howitzer was designed to attack targets deeper into the enemy rear. This included command posts, reserve units, assembly areas, and logistic facilities.

Out in the snow is a 10.5cm howitzer in a field. It was primarily the artillery regiments that were given the task of destroying enemy positions and fortified defences and conducting counter-battery fire prior to an armoured or infantry assault.

Troops of Army Group North with supplies on a sled. The Red Army looked upon their winter offensive as the last great push on the Eastern Front. The principal objective was to crush the remaining German forces in Poland, East Prussia and the Baltic states. Along the Baltic an all-out Russian assault had begun in earnest with the main intention of crushing the remaining understrength German units of the once vaunted Army Group North.

An infantry gun crew belonging to a battery of 10.5cm FH 18/40 pose for the camera. Throughout the war the 10.5cm gun provided both the Wehrmacht and Waffen-SS with a versatile, relatively mobile, base of fire.

A well concealed PaK gun in the snow. A typical strongpoint deployed along the German front comprised mainly of MG34 and MG42 machine guns, an anti-tank rifle company or battalion, a sapper platoon that was equipped with a host of various explosives, infantry guns, anti-tank artillery company which had a number of anti-tank guns, and occasionally a self-propelled gun.

Wehrmacht officers converse during operations to defend the Homeland. Whilst it appeared that the Germans were prepared for a Soviet attack, much of the equipment employed along the defensive belts was too thinly spread. Commanders were also unable to predict exactly where the strategic focal point of the Soviet attack would take place. To make matters worse when the Russians begun heavily bombing German positions all along the German frontier, this also severely weakened the strongest defensive lines.

SS troops at a field kitchen probably during operations in the Baltic region in January or February 1945. German commanders in the field now resigned themselves to the gloomy prospect of losing much of their defensive positions in the east. For them it marked the beginning of the Soviet invasion of the Fatherland. As German forces fought to delay the inevitable capture of East Prussia, and Poland, the main bulk of the Red Army drive bypassed various pockets of resistance and spilled out into eastern Pomerania, where it fought a number of hard-pressed battles.

A mortar crew engage an enemy target during a defensive action. Despite the best efforts of the German Army to bolster its dwindling ranks on the Eastern Front during the last months of the war, nothing could mask the fact that they were dwarfed by the superiority of the Red Army. It was estimated that the Russians had some six million men along a front, which stretched from the Adriatic to the Baltic.

A familiar sign in the east during the early winter of 1945. Here a column of Wehrmacht troops trudge westward along a frozen muddy road. Even by 1945 horse drawn power was still the most used form of transportation in the German Army.

A 5cm PaK 38 gun positioned on the edge of a village somewhere along the border of Poland with the Reich. Although the Germans were poorly matched in terms of equipment and supply a number of the troops were hardened veterans that had survived some of the most costly battles in the East. Hurriedly these troops were positioned along the main roads leading into Germany. Heavy machine gun platoons dug-in and held each end of the line while the remainder were scattered inside various villages and towns. Armoured vehicles, PaK and FlaK units took up key positions in order to defend the main roads.

A German soldier probably in a forward observation post communicating by radio. This soldier wears the reversible winter uniform, which was supplied to front lines troops. The uniform was not only very warm but provided the wearer with greater freedom of movement, especially with personal equipment. This uniform not only helped combat the severity of the cold, but helped prevent overheating during physical exertion.

In a dugout in the snow and a Wehrmacht mortar crew can be seen preparing their 12cm Granatwerfer 42 sGW 42 mortar. This deadly weapon, developed in direct response to encounters with the heavy Russian mortar of the same caliber; the Germans designed a virtual copy of the Red Army weapon.

Panzergrenadiers have evidently hitched a lift on board a whitewashed StuG.III Ausf.G during winter operations. Although the StuG had proven excellent against light and medium Soviet tanks at long to medium range, they were vulnerable to attacks from Soviet slit trenches, once they were separated from the heavy machine gun protection of the lighter tanks, vehicles and infantry. As a consequence losses were very high.

A battery of StuG.III Ausf.G out on the battlefield during defensive operations in the East. During the last two years of the war the assault guns had been slowly absorbed into the Panzer units, Panzer and Panzer grenadier divisions of the Wehrmacht and Waffen-SS.

A group of Wehrmacht troops pose for the camera standing in front a white washed transport vehicle.

In spite the dire situation on the front lines troops still sometimes had time to sing and bond with their comrades as this photograph clearly illustrates. Throughout February and March 1945 the Germans continued to fight a frenzied battle of attrition. In many areas where troops fought a determined defence many were encircled and annihilated.

An Sd.Kfz.251 halftrack tows a lorry through a stream during its unit's withdrawal from Poland across into the Homeland. Whilst many units withdrew under the relentless weight of the Red Army there were many isolated units that spent hours or even days fighting a bloody defence. Russian soldiers frequently requested them to surrender and assured them that no harm would come to them if they did so. But despite this reassuring tone, most German troops continued to fight to the end.

An Sd.Kfz.251 withdraws through Poland as German positions get increasingly pounded by aerial attack. Red Army commanders were well aware of the difficult task of breaking through many of the strong German defensive positions and planned to heavily rely on systematic aerial and ground bombardment. Over the next few weeks hundreds of artillery pieces were drawn-up and positioned by the Russians. In some areas there were some 250 guns per square mile.

Panzergrenadiers move across snowy terrain with a Marder Ausf. M tank destroyer following behind.. Many of the troops were already fatigued, low on ammunition and equipment and would soon be unable to defend the frontier of Poland with the Reich. Among the defenders scattered in various defensive positions, towns and villages were thousands of *Volkssturm* and *Hitlerjugend* conscripts and various other local militia and volunteers. These undertrained recruits were hastily brought in to bolster the already depleted *Wehrmacht* and *Waffen-SS* forces.

An MG34 light machine gun operator positioned in a field lying next to his feeder. Although the MG34 had by this stage of the war been augmented by the faster-firing MG42, it was still considered a very effective weapon and was used extensively in Russia until the end of the war.

A 7.5m PaK 40 crew during a lull in the defensive fighting. Along the German front lines was a mixture of troops, mortar, tanks, PaK and FlaK guns. Behind these defensive positions at varying depths were anti-tank defences, including mortars, Panzerschreck, Panzerfaust, 7.5cm and 8.8cm PaK guns, ready to counter any enemy armoured vehicle that managed to break through. However, whilst it appeared that the Germans were prepared for a Soviet attack, much of the equipment employed along the defensive belts was too thinly spread. Commanders too were unable to predict exactly where the strategic focal point of the Soviet attack would take place. To make matters worse when the Russians begun heavily bombing German positions all along the frontier, this also severely weakened the strongest defensive lines.

One of the most important forms of defensive action in any battle was communication from the front lines to the command post. Here in this photograph a radioman can be seen with his radio set communicating to one of the many field posts scattered in the rear.

A photograph of an 8.8cm FlaK gun in the snow during a defensive action in Poland in January or February 1945. In some sectors of the front, some units barely had enough Panzers to oppose the Russian armour and called upon FlaK battalions to halt the Red Army's attacks.

Foreign conscripts in a typical defensive position along the front. Undoubtedly the German soldier was stalling for time, trying their utmost to slow down the Russian drive westwards towards Berlin. Yet there seemed nothing available to him to hold-back the Soviet might, except iron will and fortitude. With determination and fanatical resistance both the German army and their foreign counterparts remained formidable opponents, fighting for every bridge, castle, town and village against the onrushing Red Army. But to the German soldier the defence of the Reich was no normal retreat. They knew very well that the Russians were determined to exact vengeance. As its army steamrolled through into Europe it left a wake of devastation.

A StuG.III Ausf.G advances along a muddy road. From 1943 until the end of the war the assault guns were slowly absorbed into the Panzer units, Panzer, and Panzergrenadier divisions of the *Wehrmacht* and *Waffen-SS*. Generally, despite the lack of fuel the StuG.III did remarkably well and fought with distinction, even in defensive actions again enemy armour.

Heavily equipped Panzergrenadiers in undergrowth during defensives actions in March 1945. They are wearing the splinter reversible padded winter jacket and trousers. This splinter pattern camouflage was printed in two shades, light and dark, with each side being made from separate pieces of the two types of camouflage cloth.

Sappers laying Teller mines during a defensive action in March 1945. Although the Germans were poorly matched in terms of equipment and supply a number of the troops were hardened veterans that had survived some of the most costly battles in the East. Hurriedly these troops were positioned along the main roads and other important areas of the front where it was thought that the Red Army would break through. Crude obstacles were then erected, and troops were emplaced in defensive positions armed with a motley assortment of anti-tank and FlaK guns, machine guns, Panzerfaust, Panzerschrek, and where possible mines fields were laid at intervals.

Operations in the Baltic and a column of vehicles including draught animals can be seen towing what remaining supplies there were at their disposal. These forces comprised of what was left of Army Group North. By the end of March the situation for Army Group North, now renamed Army of East Prussia, deteriorated further. Its forces were now hemmed in around the Bay of Danzig from Samland and Königsberg to the mouth of the Vistula. The remnants of two corps were given the task of holding positions north of Gotenhafen on the Hel Peninsula. Hitler demanded that it be held at all costs. He instructed all forces in of Army of East Prussia and Army Kurland, to stay in the front, and then held in order to draw the maximum enemy forces against itself and hopefully away from the main Soviet drive on Berlin.

A 15cm gun crew in a defensive action during the last weeks of the Battle of the Baltic States. During this period as German forces tried to maintain its unstable position in the north the Red Army pulled together its forces into three powerful fronts with the main thrust being directed against Berlin. In the north the 2.Belorussian Front was to cross the Oder north of Schwedt and strike toward Neustrelitz. Its thrust was intended to drive out the defending 3rd Panzer back against the coast and cover the advance toward Berlin on the north. German forces, however, were determined to try and hold their positions for as long as possible and prevent the Russians from taking possession of German territory. But in spite dogged resistance in many places the Germans no longer had the man power, war plant or transportation to defend their positions effectively.

An Sd.Kfz.251 halftrack tows a Horch Cross Country vehicle and a Type 82 Volkswagen Kübelwagen across muddy terrain during its unit's withdrawal somewhere in the Baltic area earlier in the war. With the capture of Danzig, Zoppot, and Gotenhafen, Hitler reluctantly conceded that the situation along the Baltic was so perilous that an invasion of the *Reich* would be imminent. Further along the coast other ports were heavily fortified in order to re-supply troops and contain the Red Armies remorseless drive.

Inside a typical dug-out on the Eastern Front. A mortar crew prepares their weapon for action. They are all wearing the reversible gray/white two-piece winter grey-side out. They blend particularly well into their surroundings.

Troops withdraw across the Vistula River during a furious withdrawal from the might of the advancing Red Army. At the end of March the military situation for the Germans in Poland had deteriorated so badly, in spite of fanatical resistance, that even Hitler himself began reluctantly allowing his forces to withdraw across the Polish frontier into the Reich where he believed they would have a better chance of defence.

A German soldier proudly stands beside a destroyed British or Canadian-built 2 pounder-armed Valentine tank. The German soldier was determined at all costs to knock out as many Red Army tanks as possible, but the constant onslaught of the massive tank armadas meant that in spite of heavy Russian losses there were always more to replace those already knocked out.

During the defence of the Reich and every weapon in the remaining German arsenal was used for its disposal. Here in this photograph among the wreckage of an urbanized battle stands a knocked out StuG.IV. Russian troops can be seen in the background.

What appear to be Hungarian POWs being led away into captivity during the loss of Hungary. The column of POWs passes a knocked out Jagdpanzer IV. The Jagdpanzer was an effective tank destroyer, but by the time it left the factory its unique defensive attributes mattered little anymore.

Chapter 3

Fighting in Front of Berlin

By the end of March the bulk of the German forces that once consisted of *Heeresgruppe Mitte*, and was now known as *Heeresgruppe* Vistula were manned by many inexperienced training units. Some soldiers were so young that in their rations they had sweets instead of tobacco. All of them were ordered to stand and fight and not to abandon their positions. Terrified at the prospect of retreating, which would warrant almost certain execution if they did so, many reluctantly opted to bury themselves deep in a foxhole or bunker. Here they hoped the Soviet attackers would give them a chance to surrender, instead of burning them alive with flamethrowers or blowing them to pieces by hand grenade.

By early April the atmosphere among the troops of *Heeresgruppe* Vistula became a mixture of terrible foreboding and despair as the Russians prepared to push forward on the River Oder. Here along the Oder and Neisse fronts the troops waited for the front to become engulfed by the greatest concentration of firepower ever amassed by the Russians. General Zhukov's 1st Belorussian Front and General Konev's 1st Ukrainian Front were preparing to attack German forces defending positions east of Berlin. For the attack the Red Army mustered some 2.5 million men, divided into four armies. They were supported by 41,600 guns and heavy mortars as well as 6,250 tanks and self-propelled guns.

The final battle before Berlin began at dawn on 16 April 1945. Just thirty-eight miles east of the German capital above the swollen River Oder, red flares burst into the night sky, triggering a massive artillery barrage. For nearly an hour, an eruption of flame and smoke burst along the German front. Then, in the mud, smoke, and darkness, the avalanche broke. In an instant, General Zhukov's soldiers were compelled to stumble forward into action. As they surged forward, the artillery barrage remained in front of them, covering the area a head.

Under the cover of darkness on the night of 15th, most German forward units had been moved back to a second line just before the expected Russian artillery barrage. Here in this defensive line troops dug-in deeply. Dozens of MG42 machine gun nests were buried along newly constructed fortified defences in order to stem advancing infantry. The MG42 was regarded by the German soldier as a formidable weapon of war and was probably the greatest machine-gun of the Second World War. As long as machine gunners could keep their machine guns operational, they were quiet capable of holding up attacking infantry many times their number. Furthermore, it only took a few well-sighted, well-hidden and well-supplied MG42 machine guns to delay an entire attacking regiment for hours on a frontage of some five or six miles.

Along with the various MG42 machine gun positions were an assortment of the 5cm PaK38, 7.5cm PaK40, the 8.8cm PaK43 and the deadly 8.8cm FlaK guns that were being used against both ground and aerial targets. These guns were the backbone of the defence against the overwhelming Soviet armour and would prove crucial in the last weeks that followed, despite a gradual depletion in ammunition.

In this second line soldiers waited for the advancing Russians. Along the entire front dispersed among the *3.* and *9.Armee's* they had fewer than 700 tanks and self-propelled guns. The heaviest division, the 25.Panzer, had just 79 such vehicles: the smallest unit had just two. Artillery too was equally poor with only 744 guns. Ammunition and fuel were in a critical state of supply and reserves in some units were almost non-existent. Opposing the main Russian assault stood the *56.Panzer-Korps*. It was under the command of General Karl Weidling, known to his friends as 'smasher Karl'. Weidling had been given the awesome task of preventing the main Russian breakthrough in the area.

When the Soviet forces finally attacked during the early morning of 16 April, the Germans were ready to meet them on the Seelow Heights. From the top of the ridge, hundreds of German FlaK guns that had been hastily transferred from the Western Front poured a hurricane of fire into the enemy troops. All morning, shells and gunfire rained down on the Red Army, blunting the assault. By dusk the Russians, savagely mauled by the attack, fell back. It seemed the Red Army had under-estimated the strength and determination of their enemy.

By the next day, the Russians had still not breached the German defences. But General Zhukov, with total disregard of casualties, was determined to batter the enemy into submission and ruthlessly bulldoze his way through. Slowly and systematically the Red Army began smashing through their opponents. Within hours hard-pressed and exhausted German troops were feeling the full brunt of the assault. Confusion soon swept the decimated lines. Soldiers who had fought doggedly from one fixed position to another were now seized with panic.

In three days of constant fighting, thousands of German soldiers perished. Despite their attempts to blunt the Red Army, the road to Berlin was finally wrenched wide open. At this crucial moment a number of top quality *SS* soldiers had been gathered in the recently established *11.Panzer-Armee* under the command of *SS-Obergruppenführer* Felix Steiner. The *11.Panzer-Armee* had been given the task of launching an offensive designed to dislocate the threatened enemy advance on Berlin, but had been halted against massive attacks. When the final push on Berlin begun on 16 April, the *11.Panzer-Armee* retained only three reliable divisions. One of these, the 18.Panzergrenadier-Division, was transferred from east of Berlin. A few days later the 11.SS.Panzergrenadier-Division 'Nordland' was rushed to Berlin and the SS Brigade 'Nederland' was sent out of the capital to help stem the Russian advance. Inside the ruined city, part of the 15.Waffengrenadier-Division der SS from Latvia was ordered to take up defensive positions together with the Belgian 'Langemarck' and 'Wallonien' Divisions, and the remaining volunteers of the French 'Charlemagne' Division. All of these *Waffen-SS* troops were to take part in the last, apocalyptic struggle to save the Reich capital from the clutches of the Red Army.

A soldier changing his clothing in the snow. He wears the reversible white camouflage trousers. The soldiers found their winter clothing extremely warm and comfortable, and provided the wearer with greater freedom of movement, especially with personal equipment. This uniform not only helped combat the severity of the cold, but helped prevent overheating during physical exertion.

A captured Jagdtiger in 1945. The Jagdtiger saw service from late 1944 to the end of the war on the *Western Front* in small numbers. The Jagdtiger was the heaviest *armoured fighting vehicle* to see service during World War II.

A Wehrmacht gun crew with their 7.5cm le IG18 light infantry artillery piece. This particular weapon was used in direct infantry support. The gun was very versatile in combat and the crew often aggressively positioned it, which usually meant the piece was regularly exposed on the battlefield. A typical infantry regiment controlled three infantry battalions, an infantry gun company with six 7.5cm le IG18. Remarkably this weapon was one of the first post World War One guns to be issued to the Wehrmacht and later the Waffen-SS. The gun was light and robust and employed a shotgun breech action. Even during the last months of the war this weapon was widely used, especially in foreign units.

Two Nebelwerfer 41's in a field. The Nebelwerfer 41 was equipped with six barrels, each firing a 34 kg (75 lb.) 150 mm (5.9 in.) Wurfgranate 41 (rocket shell 41) rocket out to a range of approximately 6800 meters (7437 yards). Along the German front the Nebelwerfer was used extensively and caused high losses in the Russian lines.

From a typical dug-out soldiers can be seen preparing their position supported by armoured vehicles. Much of the German front consisted of many miles of trenches and various other forms of defensive positions. For days Russian ground and artillery pounded the front but both the Wehrmacht and their Waffen-SS counterparts had dug deep and were determined to defend their positions to the bitter end.

A well camouflaged Panther has halted. As German troops found themselves constantly becoming either encircled or cut-off the Panthers were organized into special rescue units to relieve the trapped pockets of Germans. During the course of these daring rescue missions Panther crews fought with tenacity and courage, but time and time again the sheer weight of the Soviet army overwhelmed them.

A FlaK position along a road. Troops can be seen marching along the road supported by an Sd.Kfz.251 halftrack personnel carrier. These vehicles were used extensively during the latter half of the war to transport Panzergrenadiers to the forward edge of the battlefield. Despite being lightly armoured, they could maintain a relatively modest speed and manoeuvre across country and keep up with the fast-moving spearheads.

A halftrack advances across a field. This vehicle tows a shielded 2cm FlaK gun. By 1944 both Wehrmacht and Waffen-SS mechanized formations were well-equipped with FlaK guns, but during the last months of the war with the lack of ammunition and fuel it rendered many of them useless for combat operations.

A soldier poses for the camera standing in front of an Sd.Kfz.251 personnel carrier. On the Eastern Front the halftrack undoubtedly transformed the fighting quality of the infantry and enabled them to support the advancing armoured spearheads.

Panzergrenadiers during defensive operations in Poland. During the last two years of the war the number of Panzergrenadier divisions had grown considerably and they soon earned respect, being called the Panzer Elite. With the mounting losses of men and armour, the Panzergrenadiers displayed outstanding ability and endurance in the face of overwhelming odds. Although losses in terms of manpower and equipment had been too high in the face of increasing Russian strength, the Germans could still mount a number of small scale counterattacks.

A Wehrmacht soldier can be seen standing next to the muzzle brake of a 7.5cm gun barrel. He holds a pair of 6x30 field binoculars.

Two photographs showing a MG42 light machine gun position during a defensive operation. Although a machine gun troop was normally a three man squad, due to the high casualty rates suffered on the Eastern Front they were commonly reduced to just two, but still highly effective. Although very successful in an offensive role the MG42 was also equally as good in a defensive role too. Constantly it proved its worth time and time again.

Troops are unloading ammunition from a train which were specially packed with straw to avoid them being damaged in transit.

A Wehrmacht soldier armed with a Karbiner 98K bolt action rifle, the standard German infantry weapon used throughout the war. He is also armed with an Stg 24 grenade which has been tucked into his black leather infantryman's belt.

A gunner with his shielded 2cm FlaK gun hidden in undergrowth. Despite the size these anti-aircraft guns demonstrated outstanding anti-aircraft capabilities even during the last months of the war. By this period of operations in the east many of these weapons were being used against Russian light armour, which was also very effective.

Waffen-SS in a German town can be seen near a Volkswagen Type 166 Schwimmwagen, which literally meant Floating/Swimming Car. This amphibious four-wheel drive off-roader was used extensively by both the *Wehrmacht* and the *Waffen-SS* during on the Eastern Front. The Type 166 was the most numerous mass-produced amphibious car in history. Note the Panzerfaust carried inside the vehicle.

A photograph showing a Panzerjäger Tiger or Ferdinand Elefant tank destroyer that has been chocked and secured ready for their journey by rail. Due to their sheer size and weight, no more than six of these vehicles were permitted to be loaded on one train. These were interspersed with two flatcars to avoid overloading of the trains, and also to prevent overloading of the bridges.

Grenadiers cross a river during the final stages of the battle of the Baltic's. In a number of sectors of the front the Germans were still fighting on foreign soil, trying desperately to gain the initiative and throw back the Red Army from its remorseless drive towards the Reich frontier.

Two soldiers pose for the camera in front of one of many shelters erected along the German front in Army Group North. These shelters were called *Halbgruppenunterstände* (group and half-group living bunkers). These were to become essential for the *Landser* if they were to survive the ceaseless artillery and terrible freezing weather conditions.

Photograph showing a 15cm Nebelwerfer 41 during a fire mission. This deadly weapon fired 2.5kg shells from a six-tube mounted rocket launcher. The projectiles could fire to a maximum range of 7,000 metres. When fired the projectiles screamed through the air causing the enemy to become unnerved by the noise. These fearsome weapons that caused extensive carnage in the enemy lines served in independent army rocket launcher battalions, and in regiments and brigades.

An Sd.Kfz.10 with a mounted 2cm FlaK gun can be seen in a field. This FlaK gun had a practical rate of fire of 120 rounds-per-minute, with a maximum horizontal range of 4800 metres, which was particularly effective against both ground and aerial targets. A number of these mounted FlaK guns were used in the defensive actions in both Poland and the Reich in a desperate attempt to help in the delay of the Russian onslaught. However, like so many German vehicles employed in the East, they were too few or dispersed to make any significant impact on the main Soviet operations which were already capturing or encircling many of the key towns and cities.

A halted Panther in Poland. During the bitter fighting in Poland the Panther was used extensively to thwart the sheer weight of the Russian drive. As German troops found themselves constantly becoming either encircled or cut-off the Panthers were organized into special rescue units to relieve the trapped pockets of Germans. During the course of these daring rescue missions Panther crews fought with tenacity and courage, but time and time again the sheer weight of the Soviet army overwhelmed them. Although many Panthers were lost in action as a result of these brave rescue missions, it was the lack of fuel and ammunition that eventually forced these lethal machines to a standstill.

Following contact with the enemy three grenadiers can be seen resting before resuming defensive operations. In the distance smoke can be seen rising into the air indicating that a position has hit by shelling.

A Waffen-SS squad leader gropes his way through a forested area. His armed with the 9mm MP38/40, one of the most effective submachine guns produced during World War Two.

A *Waffen-SS* mortar crew pose for the camera in their dug-out position. By this period of the war the German soldier had expended considerable effort, but lacked sufficient reconnaissance and the necessary support of tanks and heavy weapons to compensate for the large losses sustained.

Waffen-SS s.IG33 15cm artillery gun being used in action. A typical infantry regiment controlled three infantry battalions, an infantry gun company with six 7.5cm l.IG18 and two 15cm s.IG33 guns, and an anti-tank company with twelve 3.7cm PaK35/36 guns. The 15cm s.IG33 infantry gun was regarded the workhorse pieces operated by specially trained infantrymen. Whilst these artillery pieces were effective at destroying enemy positions they were not very good at halting enemy armour. During the Russian advance through Poland and the Baltic States the Germans found it very difficult to contain the Soviet onslaught. As a result many parts of the front were beginning to disintegrate. Already it had incurred thousands of casualties trying to contain the Soviets. Totally exhausted and unable to hold back the enemy for any appreciable length of time, Hitler still prohibited all voluntary withdrawals and reserved all decisions to withdraw himself. In a leadership conference held by the *Führer* the commanders were told to infuse determination in their men and to strengthen faith in ultimate victory. But in spite of Hitler's radical measures in trying to generate the will to fight until success was secured, the German Army were unable to stop the advancing Russian forces.

Wearing winter whites in early 1945, this grenadier is armed with the most powerful and effective machine of the Second World War, the MG42. Whilst the German front continued to fight with fanatical resistance, it came with a high price in men and materials. However, the German soldier was still capable of meeting the highest standards, fighting courageously with self-sacrifice against massive numerical superiority.

Two Wehrmacht troops in a dug-out during defensive operations. One way of avoiding getting killed out in the open was to dig a hole and lay inside until the enemy either changed its direction of fire or were beaten back.

Assault troops go into action in the snow with a mortar attack. Attacking an enemy position was frequently very hazardous, and prior to any major assault mortar, artillery or air bombardment was often required to allow infantry and armour to move forward to reduce significant casualties.

A 2cm Flak gun mounted on the back of a half track on a road during a defensive operation. The sides of the vehicle are folded down. The sides allowed extra space on board the halftrack for the crew to move about more easily. Note the light MG34 machine gunner in action. This light MG is being used from its bipod mount. With the bipod extended and the belt loaded, the machine gunner could effectively move the weapon quickly from one position to another and throw it to the ground and put it into operation, with deadly effect.

During a lull in the fighting a group of Waffen-SS troops share a packet of cigarettes. One of the soldiers is holding a bag more than likely containing some rations. The troops were issued a march ration of sausage, cheese, dried bread, coffee, and sugar in paper bags. However, during the last months of the war, almost all rations had been exhausted and many troops had to rely on scavenging for what they could find, either from dead comrades, civilians, or captured stocks.

Panzergrenadiers support the advance of a Jagdpanzer IV during the last months of the war. With the drastic need for new armoured fighting vehicles more second generation tank destroyers were built. One such vehicle that came off the production line in 1944 was the Jagdpanzer IV. This vehicle built on the chassis of a Pz.Kpfw.IV weighed 28.5 tons. The vehicle was equal to any enemy tanks thanks to its potent 7.5cm gun. The Jagdpanzer saw extensive service in the east and with its reliability and well sloped thick frontal armour it became a highly efficient fighting vehicle. In the foreground is a Soviet 7.62cm field gun in German use.

A Waffen-SS crew with their 7.5cm PaK40's during a fire mission. The PaK40 effectiveness on the battlefield made it a very popular weapon with both the Wehrmacht and Waffen-SS, but there were never enough of them to meet the ever-increasing demand on the Eastern Front. Throughout its life on the battlefield the PaK40 was a powerful and deadly weapon, especially in the hands of well-trained anti-tank gunners.

Two Panzergrenadiers watch as a building burns after evidently coming aerial or ground bombardment. During the last two years of the war Germany was continually bombed by both American and British bomber squadrons, and as the Red Army neared the frontier of the Reich in late 1944, they also took part in extensive aerial attacks.

Six photographs showing various troops armed with the deadly Panzerfaust. During the last year of the war the Panzerfaust was used extensively to combat Russian armour. It was a handheld rocket-propelled grenade, which was effective at a range of about 90-feet. The weapon had a total weight of 5.1 kilograms and total length of 1.045 metres. The launch tube was made of low-grade steel containing a 95-gram charge of black powder propellant. Along the side of the tube were a simple folding rear sight and a trigger. The edge of the warhead was used as the front sight. The oversize warhead was fitted into the front of the tube by an attached wooden tail stem with metal stabilizing fins. The warhead weighed 2.9 kilograms and contained 0.8 kilograms of a 50:50 mixture of TNT and hexogen explosives, and had armour penetration of 200 millimetres. This weapon became very effective against enemy tanks during the last months of the war and as a result of their effectiveness on the battlefield some tank units often waited for infantry support before advancing in order to minimize the risk of being knocked out. The high kill rate by the Panzerfaust, however, is attributed mainly by the lack of German anti-tank guns late in the war and also the terrain where the fighting took place.

Wehrmacht commanders stand in front of a command vehicle somewhere on the Eastern Front. By this period of the war many commanders were in no doubt of the seriousness of the military situation and began taking steps to safeguard their units from complete annihilation.

A decorated soldier poses for the camera with his Iron Cross.

A mortar crew inside a well dug-in 8cm sGrW 34 mortar position. Life in the line for these soldiers was a continuous grind, but any let-up in defence would ensure that the Red Army would push deeper into the German defences. German commanders in the field were well aware of the disasters befalling their comrades in the central and southern sectors of the front, and knew that their position in Poland was becoming more precarious with each passing day.

Two photographs showing a captured Russian 76.2cm PaK39 being used in a defensive role. Captured Russian weapons like this were used extensively by the Germans during the war and allowed depleted units to be brought up to relative strength.

A Panzergrenadier holding a pair of 6x30 field binoculars can be seen in a field. He wears a green splinter army reversible camouflage tunic.

A StuG halted at the side of the road. Despite their lethal 75mm guns, these assault guns were continually hard-pressed on the battlefield and constantly called upon for offensive and defensive fire support, where they were gradually compelled to operate increasingly in an anti-tank role. As a direct result of this many of them were lost in battle.

A *Luftwaffe* 2cm FlaK gun position in a field. The number of guns assigned to light FlaK batteries varied through the war, but was typically twelve 2cm and/or 3.7cm guns in four platoons.

A StuG has halted on a road and the crew can be seen posing for the camera. By 1944 the StuG had become an extremely common assault gun, especially on the Eastern Front. By this period of the war the StuG had been slowly absorbed into Panzer units, Panzer and Panzergrenadier divisions of the Wehrmacht and Waffen-SS. Even during the last months of the war the StuG done sterling service against overwhelming superiority.

Here a Sturmapanzer IV Brummbär during deployment for action. At Hitler's insistence an assault howitzer for use in urban combat was produced and the body was constructed on the chassis of a Pz.Kpfw.IV. The Brümmbar or 'Grizzly bear' as it was nicknamed, mounted the powerful s.IG 15cm gun. In early August 1944 10 Sturmpanzer's were transferred to Army Group Centre to assist in the Warsaw uprising.

Halted on a road are two Flakpanzer IV Wirbelwind (Whirlwind). This Panzer variant was armed with quad 2cm anti-aircraft cannons. Some 100 of them were built but made little impact on the battlefield.

A Waffen-SS 10.5cm heavy field howitzer during a fire mission. Even during the withdrawal combat experience soon showed that artillery support was of decisive importance in both defensive and offensive roles.

A 3.7cm FlaK 18 gun. Aerial attacks across the German front were merciless and often unceasing for many hours. The Soviet Air Force caused unprecedented amounts of destruction to German columns and defensive positions. Here in this photograph young FlaK gunners have been conscripted into the defence of the Reich.

Chapter 4

The End

In the first two weeks of April German forces along the entire front from the north to the south tried to maintain their unstable position. In the north the Red Army pulled together its forces into three powerful fronts with the main effort being directed against Berlin. In the north the 2.Belorussian Front was to cross the Oder north of Schwedt and strike toward Neustrelitz. Its thrust was intended to drive out the defending *3.Panzer-Armee* back against the coast and cover the advance toward Berlin on the north. German forces, however, were determined to try and hold their positions for as long as possible and prevent the Russians from taking possession of German territory. But despite dogged resistance in many places the Germans no longer had the man power, equipment or transportation to defend their positions effectively. The *3.Panzer-Armee* had 11 remaining divisions, whilst the 2. Belorussian Front had 8 armies totalling 33 rifle divisions, 4 tank and mechanized corps, and 3 artillery divisions plus a mixture of artillery and rocket launcher brigades and regiments. The Germans were dwarfed by enemy superiority but continued to fight from one fixed position to another.

By mid-April the 2.Belorussian Front had successfully pushed back the *3.Panzer-Armee* and had taken a bridgehead ten miles long above the city of Stettin. Inside Stettin the city had been turned into a fortress and was being defended by 'Fortress Division Stettin'. It was formed out of parts of the *3.Panzer-Armee* and during its defensive battle it put up staunch resistance.

All along the receding Eastern Front Hitler gathered his commanders and told them the outcome of the war would be decided before Berlin. He outlined it was for this reason his brave legions would have to fight to save their Homeland from a Soviet invasion. Yet the average German soldier held a grim conviction that the war was lost, and yet there was still no end in sight. Being always outnumbered, perpetually short of fuel and ammunition, and having to constantly exert themselves and their machinery to the very limits of endurance had a profound effect on life at the front. The equipment situation had deteriorated too, especially in the Panzer units. The effect of depleting the experienced and elite formations like the *Waffen-SS* was a constant concern for the tacticians. The *SS* did receive a high proportion of tanks, artillery and assault guns, but this was in stark contrast to the enormous volume of armaments being produced by the Russians. The *SS* were thus faced with a dangerous and worsening prospect, but unlike the normal German soldier many of these elite troops retained their fanatical determination on the battlefield.

As *Waffen-SS* and *Wehrmacht* forces established defensive lines in the face of the advancing enemy, commanders looked to the aggressive and loyal striking force of the *SS* and counted on them to snatch victory from defeat, but even the *SS* were severely worn down by constant fighting. A feeling of despair and gloom prevailed across the entire German Army. But in spite this deep concern of a looming defeat the German soldier fought on. The situation for the defenders was calamitous. The Germans were well aware how important it was to prevent the Russians breaking across in to the Homeland, but there seemed no stopping the Red Army drive. Panzergrenadiers, *Luftwaffe* field units, *Waffen-SS*, *Hitlerjugend* and *Volkssturm* conscripts tried in vain to hold back the enemy onslaught, but they could not withstand the overwhelming superiority. As a result of the constant fighting the front line along the Reich was finally wrenched open and Russian troops spewed through whilst German forces withdrew westward.

There were now only two main German armies left remaining holding the front less than 100 miles east of Berlin. German panzer and infantry troops were compelled to hold the front against superior Soviet artillery and aviation. In that sector, most of the front lay on the western bank of the Oder, there were two major bridgeheads still on the eastern bank: in the north, the historic town of the Stettin; to the south, the city of Frankfurt-on-Oder. Both sat opposite Berlin. There were two armies holding the front to prevent the Russians from continuing their drive and capturing the German capital. On the northern wing was the *3.Panzer-Armee*. Eighty miles south was the *9.Armee* under the faithful command of General Theodor Busse. From one collapsed sector of the front to another, the force of some 250,000 men had slowly withdrawn to the Oder. Over the weeks Busse's force had taken the full brunt of the Russian attacks, and was slowly wilting under the constant hammer blows of enemy artillery. Yet the *9.Armee* was still defiantly holding in a number of places.

At Frankfurt, they had actually thrown back the enemy. Although mercilessly bombed and shelled at Seelow, the men had doggedly and persistently pinned the enemy down. But their ardent defensive tactics had cost them dearly.

On 15 April, Hitler sent an Order of the Day directly to the *9.Armee*'s headquarters to appeal to the soldiers to stand fast. What the *Führer* was actually requesting was for every man to fight to the death. However, within a few days of Hitler's Stand Fast order the Red Army had broken through in two places and began approaching Berlin. The *9.Armee* was between the two massive Russian pincers that were heading for the capital. Losses for the Germans were huge and Busse was facing a major catastrophe, and yet the General still did not consider pulling back. Retreat, except under orders, was comparable to treason. Hitler's orders were to stand fast at all costs. With the *9.Armee* denied any freedom of movement, it was certain to be destroyed. Despite constant appeals from commanders in the field 'to act now in order to save *9.Armee* from destruction', Hitler's stubborn hold order remained the same. From the *Führer* headquarters, which was now entombed 60 feet below the ravaged streets of Berlin, a message was sent to Busse sealing the fate of his army: '*The 9.Armee must hold its position. At the same time, all forces should be made available to try and close the gap with Schorner on the southern flank so as to set up a continuous front once more*'.

By 22 April, Busse's force was almost encircled and close to annihilation. In spite of orders from Hitler headquarters that the line of defence of the Order must never be abandoned, Busses with the larger half of the *9.Armee* comprising of some 80,000 troops began to withdraw south-westwards towards the Spreewald in an attempt to link up with the *12.Armee*.

Within days, the *9.Armee*, still doggedly battling towards Wenck's forces, were totally surrounded and being hammered night and day by Russian bombers. It did not take long before the entire northern flank of the army collapsed. The remnants of the army then shuffled along roads, tracks and fields trying to escape the slaughter. During their tortuous journey, the exhausted troops moved into a forest near the large village of Halbe. It was here that remnants of *9.Armee* would endure what most of the survivors called 'the slaughter of Halbe'.

North of the forest, as Busse's forces tried in vain to stave off destruction inside the Halbe forest, fighting increased as Soviet forces closed on Berlin.

By 25 April Berlin was completely surrounded, and the next day some half a million Soviet troops bulldozed their way through the city. Beneath the *Reich* Chancellery building, the *Führer* was determined to save the crumbling capital and had already ordered remnants of SS-*Obergruppenführer* Felix Steiner's *11.Panzer-Armee* to attack immediately from their positions in the Eberswalde, then to drive south, cutting off the Russian assault on Berlin. On Hitler's map, the plan looked brilliant. But it was impossible to gather forces to make Steiner's *SS Kampfgruppe* even remotely operational. Steiner himself wrote that the forces at his disposal amounted to less than a weak *Korps*. He was well aware that his attack would receive little or no support as the *9.Armee* was completely surrounded and the *12.Armee* consisted only of a few battered divisions. As for Hitler's reinforcements, they consisted of fewer than 5,000 *Luftwaffe* personnel and *Hitlerjugend*, all armed with hand-held weapons. The city was doomed.

For the next week the battle for Berlin raged. True to their motto, 'My Honour is my Loyalty', the *Waffen-SS* were seen fighting bitterly with members of the *Hitlerjugend*, *Volkssturm*, *Luftwaffe* and *Wehrmacht* troops. Here the soldiers were ordered to fight to the death and anyone found deserting or shirking from their duties was hunted down by *Reichsführer* Heinrich Himmler's personal Escort battalion and hanged from the nearest lamp post. But even in the last days of the war both the Wehrmacht and the SS proved to be an efficient, formidable and ruthless fighting machine. Even as the last hours were fought out in the fiery cauldron of Berlin, German units, lacking all provisions including many types of weapons, effectively halted and stemmed a number of Russian assaults.

Throughout the final days of the Reich Hitler was obsessed with the belief that fanatical aggression could win victories. In a number of areas his hard line strategy actually worked, but at a huge cost in men and material. Nevertheless, the hard pressed battles fought in front of the capital essentially slowed the Russian drive and tied down an immeasurable amount of men and armour. It also prevented much of the Soviet Army from reaching the Baltic Sea, which the Germans believed would seriously curtail the U-boat training programme. The Baltic Sea had also been used throughout the war to ferry vital supplies to Army Group North, and without this important supply artery operations would have seriously been hampered. Hitler made it clear that it was imperative that the troops held the front and wage a static battle of attrition until other parts of the Russian front could be stabilized.

Geographically the battle east of Berlin was an important defensive operation for the Germans. Every soldier was made aware of the significance of holding on to as much land as possible, and it was essential that they wage a static battle of attrition until other parts of the Eastern Front could be stabilized. However, slowly and systematically the Soviet Army ground down the Germans forcing its army to withdraw deeper into the Reich and fight a determined defence wherever it could. When the last German troops were finally expunged from Russian and Baltic soil, the Red Army hailed themselves as the conquerors of fascism. Now they had to drive into Germany and take Berlin. The battle for the Reich capital was a massive undertaking for the Russians and the loss of life on both sides was immense. There are no exact casualty figures, but it is reckoned that some one million men were killed and wounded just in April alone.

Following the surrender of Berlin on 2 May 1945, the will to fight of the remaining forces still attempting to defend parts of eastern Germany, notably the scattered remnants of what was left of Army Group Vistula, quickly came to an end.

Wenck's 12.Armee had begun to withdraw southwest of Potsdam and by the morning of 1 May it had taken some 30,000 survivors from Busse's 9.Armee through its line. Miraculously remnants of both army groups had escaped the impending slaughter against the strongest of Russian concentrations around Berlin and had trudged westward with the sole intention of surrendering their exhausted and badly depleted forces to the US 9th Army.

Grenadier-Regiment 1944

Regiments-Stab	
Nachrichtenzug	
Pionierzug	6 x light MG34/42
Reiter- oder Radfahrerzug	3 x light MG34/42
Grenadier-Bataillon (x2)	
Bataillons-Stab	
Schutzen-Kompanie (x3)	16 x light MG, 2 x 8cm mortar
Maschinengewehr Kompanie	3 x light MG, 12 xheavy MG, 4 x 8cm mortar
Leichte Infanterie Kolonne	
Infanteriegeschutz-Kompanie	5 x light MG, 6 x 7.5cm inf gun
	2 x 15cm inf gun
Panzerjäger-Kompanie	13 x light MG, 12 x 7.5cm AT gun
Regiments Tross	

Volksgrenadier-Regiment 1944/45

Regiments-Stab	
Stabs-Kompanie	10 x light MG34/42
Grenadier-Bataillon (x2)	
Bataillons-Stab	
Versorgungszug	2 x light MG34/42
Grenadier-Kompanie (x3)	9 x light MG
	6 x 7.5cm inf gun, 6 x 8cm mortar
Infanteriegeschutz-Kompanie	5 x light MG, 4 x 7.5cm in gun, 8 x 12cm mortar
Panzerzerstörer-Kompanie	4 x light MG
	54 x Panzerschreck
Regiment Tross	

Grenadier-Regiment 1945

Regiments-Stab	
Stabs-Kompanie	10 x light MG
Greandier-Bataillon (x2)	
Bataillons-Stab	
Versorgungszug	2 x light MG
Grenadier-Kompanie (x3)	9 x light MG
Schwere Kompanie	1 x light MG, 8 heavy MG, 4 x 7.5cm inf gun, 6 x 8cm Mortar
Schwerer Kompanie	5 x light MG, 2 x 15cm inf gun, 8 x 12cm mortar
Panzerzerstorer-Kompanie	4 x light MG, 54 x Panzerschreck (+ 18 in reserve)
Regiments Tross	

A knocked out Tiger tank on the road to Berlin in 1945. With too few of them delivered, Tigers, Panthers, assault guns and tank destroyer crews found that they were too thinly stretched to make any considerable dent against the growing tank might of the Red Army.

A well dug-in Jagdpanzer 38 (t) Hetzer tank destroyer has been well camouflaged by harvesting some kind of crop and applying it over much of the vehicle. It was imperative for armoured crews to reduce the risk of being attacked by heavily camouflaging their vehicles.

East Prussian Volkssturm personnel swear an oath of allegiance to Hitler in November 1944. The majority of them are armed with the Panzerfaust, whilst one soldier is armed with the *Panzerschreck*. (Marcin Kaludow Archive)

Two Wehrmacht soldiers move back following intensive action. The leading soldier is armed with a side arm in one have and an entrenching tool in the other. His comrade behind him who is probably a squad leader is armed with the MP38/40 submachine gun.

A 10.5cm heavy field howitzer during a fire mission. Even during the last months of the war combat experience showed that artillery support was of decisive importance in both defensive and offensive roles. It was primarily the artillery regiments that were given the task of destroying enemy positions and fortified defences and conducting counter-battery fire prior to an armoured assault.

Three photographs showing soldiers armed with the lethal *Panzerschreck* or tank shock. The popular name given by the troops for this weapon was the *Raketenpanzerbuchse* or rocket tank rifle, abbreviated to RPzB. It was an 8.8.cm reusable anti-tank rocket launcher developed during the latter half of the war. Another popular nickname was *Ofenrohr* or stove pipe.

A photograph showing a pioneer attacking an enemy position. Heavily fortified positions were often heavily defended and were frequently put out of action by determined German assault pioneers. Pioneer troops were mainly employed as assault troops to supplement the infantry. Their task involved clearing minefields, breached obstacles and attacked fortifications with demolitions and flamethrowers.

Panzergrenadiers armed with *Panzerfaust* projectors march along the side of the road followed by two Sd.Kfz.251/9s armed with the 7.5cm short barreled gun.

Two photographs showing Wehrmacht soldiers armed with a *Panzerfaust* anti-tank projector. This recoilless projector consisted of a small, disposable preloaded launch tube firing a high explosive anti-tank warhead, operated by a single soldier. The *Panzerfaust* remained in service in various versions until the end of the war. The weapon often had warnings written in large red letters on the upper rear end of the tube, warning the user of the back blast. After firing, the tube was discarded, making the Panzerfaust the first disposable anti-tank weapon.

Despite overwhelming superiority of the enemy the Germans still fought fiercely and determinedly, especially during urban fighting. Here in this photograph a squad leader armed with a MP38/40 sub-machine gun has captured a group of Russian soldiers during heavy intensive fighting inside a town.

A soldier stands on the corner of a road and watches a Panther tank slowly taking up a position inside a town. Following the battle of Stalingrad in late 1942 the Germans had become masters of urban fighting and could hold up an attacking force for many hours, days, or even weeks.

An MG34 machine gun crew passes a destroyed building during bitter fighting. An MG34 machine gunner can be seen with his weapon slung over his shoulder. The vast majority of distances travelled by the infantry were done on foot. This was often exhausting for the soldiers, especially when they were compelled to fight before or after reaching their destination.

Here a well camouflaged Ferdinand Elefant has run out of fuel. This tank destroyer was capable of defeating all types of Soviet tanks, but the vehicle lacked cross-country mobility and were prone to breakdowns.

A destroyed or abandoned Hetzer 7.5cm tank destroyer somewhere in eastern Europe.

A Jagdpanzer IV armed with a powerful 7.5cm gun barrel. Marching alongside on foot are grenadiers armed with the Panzerfaust. These Panzer IV/70 reached the Panzer units in small number until the end of the war.

Troops in a typical trench system during defensive actions along the front lines. The earth was often thrown by shovel to the front of the trench in order to create a high protective wall of defence. Planks to support the sides were often erected in unstable soil and to prevent it from being collapsed by nearby artillery strikes. As the war drew to the last remaining weeks there was almost no respite on the front line and the dwindling numbers of soldiers to man the already over extended front was causing unprecedented problems.

A British soldier surveyors a knocked out Tiger.I's which has a full application of zimmerit anti-mine paste. During the war, these vehicles constantly demonstrated both the effectiveness of their 8.8cm guns and their invulnerability to Soviet anti-tank projectiles smaller than 8.5cm. However, there were too few to make any significant advancement against their enemy.

Grenadiers, one armed with a Panzerfaust and the other a standard German infantry rifle, stand beside a tank during the last months of the war on the Eastern Front.

Soviet artillery in action against a German position. The 122mm howitzer M1938 saw extensive action on the Eastern Front mainly as a divisional artillery piece of the Red Army. Captured guns were also employed later by the Wehrmacht and the Finnish Army.

A foreign General decorates one of his men for bravery in the field during the battle for the Baltic States. It was here in the Baltic States of Estonia, Latvia and Lithuania where German forces and their remaining allied troops tried desperately to prevent the Red Army from spilling across into northern Germany and driving on to Berlin.

A photograph showing a soldier getting decorated for his courageous attempts to stem the mighty Soviet forces from breaking through the German lines during the last months of the war.

Troops take refuge in one of many bunker systems that littered the front lines. Often these bunkers were constructed quickly out of wood and afforded little in the way of protection against artillery. However, it did offer soldiers protection against machine gun and small arms fire.

One of the key areas of defence was along main roads. Here an 8.8cm FlaK crew have positioned there gun near to a road to defend the position against advancing ground forces. Note how the crew have purposely avoided positioning the gun on the road.

Whilst the StuH with 10.5cm howitzer proved its worth on the battlefield in spite its dwindling numbers, other forces supporting the vehicle were poorly supplied or lacked the equipment to deal with the enemy. As a consequence these assault guns frequently assisted the dwindling front lines, but it was invariably swamped by overwhelming Russian forces. Losses were massive.

Scraping the barrel – two photograph showing newly conscripted *Volkssturm* during the last weeks of the war. Members of the *Volkssturm* only received very basic training and there was also a serious lack of trainers, which meant many of them went to the front barely able to use their weapons properly. The majority of them were armed with either the Karabiner 98K bolt action rifle or the Panzerfaust, as in these photographs. It was often down to these men to help defend towns and villages from the onrushing enemy forces. Quite regularly *Volkssturm* conscripts threw down their arms as the attacking forces approached and went into hiding. However, there were some that fought to the death, but still rarely held back the Russian forces for any appreciable time.

With Soviet aircraft now ruling the skies in the East many German divisions had increased their anti-aircraft battalions, with each of them containing two or even three heavy batteries. In this photograph it shows an 8.8cm FlaK gun complete with *Schützchild* (protective shield). In some sectors of the front, some units barely had enough Panzers to oppose the Russian armour and called upon FlaK battalions to halt the Red Army's attacks. During this later period many FlaK guns came to be assigned dual purposes, which involved adding an anti-tank role to their operational duties. Note the kill rings on the barrel of this 8.8cm FlaK gun.

A captured Jagtiger on a Gotha 80 tonne trailer being prepared to be taken to England for inspection. Although the fire power of the Jagdtiger was lethal, its mobility was restricted mainly due to fuel shortages and mechanical breakdowns. They were also very slow moving and a relatively easy target for fighter-bombers. This is a non-standard version with experimental Porsche suspension.

Two soldiers fighting inside a rubble strewn town during defensive actions in 1945. Both troops appear to be conscripts. Whilst these conscripts had a considerable lack of experience on the battlefield Red Army troops still encountered considerable resistance in a number of areas. In front of Berlin for instance there were a number of *Hitlerjugend*, *Volkssturm*, and other militia forces that attacked wherever and whenever they could, despite the tactical futility of their actions.

Troops move along a railway line passing what appears to be a well camouflaged gun train. In spite the staunch resistance put-up by the Germans nothing could prevent the enemy onslaught.

When the Russians finally bulldozed their way into Berlin in April 1945, they flamed, bombarded and machine gunned the defenders, crushing them into the piles of rubble that littered the city. Where the Germans put up a determined resistance, the whole area was saturated by Katyusha rocket fire, as in this photograph. Note the metal blast covers protecting the vehicles windshields.

Appendix

Army Order of Battle 1945

(26 Jan 1945)
Armeegruppe Heinrici

154. Feldausbildungs-Division
1. Skijäger-Division (in transit)
Headquarters Hungarian 1st Army
Hungarian V Corps
XVII. Armeekorps
208. Infanterie-Division
Kampfgruppe 3. Gebirgs-Division
Hungarian 24th Infantry Division
Hungarian 1st Mountain Brigade (remnants)
XXXXIX. Gebirgs-Armeekorps

Hungarian 16th Infantry Division
Hungarian 2nd Field Replacement Division
254. Infanterie-Division
Kampfgruppe 4. Gebirgs-Division
XI. SS-Armeekorps
Hungarian 5th Reserve Division
Kampfgruppe 253. Infanterie-Division
320. Volks-Grenadier-Division
545. Volks-Grenadier-Division

Order of battle (1 Mar 1945)

154. Feldausbildungs-Division
18. SS-Freiwilligen-Panzergrenadier-Division
   "Horst Wessel"
XXXXIX. Gebirgs-Armeekorps
Kampfgruppe 320. Volks-Grenadier-Division
4. Gebirgs-Division
Kampfgruppe 78. Volks-Sturm-Division
545. Volks-Grenadier-Division
3. Gebirgs-Division
Hungarian 16th Infantry Division
LIX. Armeekorps
Kampfgruppe 544. Volks-Grenadier-Division
253. Infanterie-Division

Kampfgruppe 75. Infanterie-Division
68. Infanterie-Division
XI. Armeekorps
Kampfgruppe 1. Skijäger-Division
97. Jäger-Division
Kampfgruppe 371. Infanterie-Division
18. SS-Freiwilligen-Panzergrenadier-Division
   "Horst Wessel"
Kampfgruppe 344. Infanterie-Division
Korpsgruppe Schlesien
Kampfgruppe 168. Infanterie-Division
20. Waffen-Grenadier-Division der SS
   (estnische Nr. 1)

Order of battle (12 Apr 1945)

1. Panzerarmee
154. Infanterie-Division
8. Panzer-Division

75. Infanterie-Division (refitting)
17. Panzer-Division
XXXXIX. Gebirgs-Armeekorps

320. Volks-Grenadier-Division
Gruppe Oberst Bader
304. Infanterie-Division
Hungarian 16th Infantry Division
253. Infanterie-Division
3. Gebirgs-Division
LIX. Armeekorps
4. Gebirgs-Division
715. Infanterie-Division
19. Panzer-Division
16. Panzer-Division
544. Volks-Grenadier-Division

XI. Armeekorps
68. Infanterie-Division
371. Infanterie-Division
97. Jäger-Division
I. Skijäger-Division
158. Infanterie-Division
XXIV. Panzerkorps
10. Panzer-Grenadier-Division
78. Volks-Sturm-Division
254. Infanterie-Division
344. Infanterie-Division

Order of battle (30 Apr 1945)

304. Infanterie-Division
XXIV. Panzerkorps
6. Panzer-Division
8. Panzer-Division
Panzer-Division "Feldherrnhalle 1"
Kampfgruppe 711. Infanterie-Division
Kampfgruppe 182. Infanterie-Division
Kampfgruppe 46. Volks-Grenadier-Division
10. Fallschirmjger-Division (in transit)
XXIX. Armeekorps
8. Jäger-Division
19. Panzer-Division
271. Infanterie-Division
LXXII. Armeekorps
Kampfgruppe 76. Infanterie-Division
Kampfgruppe 15. Infanterie-Division
Sperr-Verband 601
Kampfgruppe 153. Infanterie-Division
XXXXIX. Gebirgs-Armeekorps
320. Volks-Grenadier-Division

253. Infanterie-Division
Hungarian 16th Infantry Division
Gruppe General Klatt
3. Gebirgs-Division
97. Jäger-Division
LIX. Armeekorps
715. Infanterie-Division
544. Volks-Grenadier-Division
371. Infanterie-Division
75. Infanterie-Division
78. Volks-Sturm-Division
154. Infanterie-Division
XI. Armeekorps
4. Gebirgs-Division
10. Panzer-Grenadier-Division
16. Panzer-Division
254. Infanterie-Division
17. Panzer-Division
158. Infanterie-Division

Order of battle (1 Mar 1945)

2. Panzerarmee
Grenadier-Brigade (mot) 92
LXVIII. Armeekorps
13. Waffen-Gebirgs-Division der SS
   "Handschar" (kroatische Nr. 1)

71. Infanterie-Division
XXII. Gebirgs-Armeekorps
I. Volks-Gebirgs-Division
118. Jäger-Division

Order of battle (12 Apr 1945)

LXVIII. Armeekorps
13. Waffen-Gebirgs-Division der SS
  "Handschar" (kroatische Nr. 1)
71. Infanterie-Division
297. Infanterie-Division
XXII. Gebirgs-Armeekorps
118. Jäger-Division
9. SS-Panzer-Division "Hohenstaufen"
I. Kavallerie-Korps

23. Panzer-Division
4. Kavallerie-Division
Kampfgruppe Reichsgrenadier-Division
  Hoch- und Deutschmeister
3. Kavallerie-Division
14. Waffen-Grenadier-Division der SS
(ukrainische Nr.1)
16. SS-Panzergrenadier-Division
  "Reichsführer SS"

Order of battle (30 Apr 1945)

13. Waffen-Gebirgs-Division der SS
  "Handschar" (kroatische Nr. 1)
71. Infanterie-Division
118. Jäger-Division
XXII. Gebirgs-Armeekorps
297. Infanterie-Division
Hungarian Szent-László Division

I. Kavallerie-Korps
23. Panzer-Division
4. Kavallerie-Division
3. Kavallerie-Division
16. SS-Panzergrenadier-Division
  "Reichsführer SS"

Order of battle (26 Jan 1945)

3. Panzerarmee
Fallschirm-Panzergrenadier-Division 2
  "Hermann Göring"
Fallschirm-Panzerkorps "Hermann Göring"
21. Infanterie-Division
50. Infanterie-Division
61. Infanterie-Division
349. Volks-Grenadier-Division
549. Volks-Grenadier-Division
56. Infanterie-Division
1. Infanterie-Division

10. Radfahr-Jäger-Brigade
5. Panzer-Division
69. Infanterie-Division
IX. Armeekorps
561. Volks-Grenadier-Division
548. Volks-Grenadier-Division
286. Infanterie-Division
XXVIII. Armeekorps
Divisionsstab. 607
58. Infanterie-Division
95. Infanterie-Division

Order of battle (1 Mar 1945)

33. Waffen-Grenadier-Division der SS
  "Charlemagne" (franz. Nr. 1)
Panzer-Division "Holstein"
Verteidigungsbereich Order
(Stellvertretendes II. Armeekorps)
9. Fallschirmjäger-Division

Gruppe Denecke
III. SS-Panzerkorps
281. Infanterie-Division
11. SS-Freiwilligen-Panzergrenadier-Division
  "Nordland"

28. SS-Freiwilligen-Grenadier-Division
  "Wallonien"
Gruppe Voigt
27. SS-Freiwilligen-Grenadier-Division
  "Langemark"
23. SS-Freiwilligen-Panzergrenadier-Division
  "Nederland" (niederlandische Nr. 1)
XI. SS-Armeekorps
5. Jäger-Division

Divisionsstab z.b.V. 402
163. Infanterie-Division
Korpsgruppe Tettau
Division Bärwalde
Division Pommerland
33. Waffen-Grenadier-Division der SS
  "Charlemagne" (franz. Nr. 1)
15. Waffen-Grenadier-Division der SS
  (lettische Nr.1) (remnants)

Order of battle (12 Apr 1945)

III. SS-Panzerkorps
11. SS-Freiwilligen-Panzergrenadier-Division
  "Nordland"
23. SS-Freiwilligen-Panzergrenadier-Division
  "Nederland" (niederlandische Nr. 1)
28. SS-Freiwilligen-Grenadier-Division
  "Wallonien"
27. SS-Freiwilligen-Grenadier-Division
  "Langemark"
XXXXVI. Panzerkorps
1. Marine-Infanterie-Division
547. Volks-Grenadier-Division

Korps Oder
Gruppe Major Klossek
Divisionsstab z.b.V. 610
XXXII. Armeekorps
281. Infanterie-Division
Festung Stettin
549. Volks-Grenadier-Division
Gruppe Generalmajor Voigt
Verteidigungsbereich Swinemünde
3. Marine-Infanterie-Division
Seekommandant Swinemünde
Ausbildungs-Division 402

Order of battle (26 Jan 1945)

4. Panzerarmee
100. Jäger-Division
VIII. Armeekorps

Kampfgruppe 168. Infanterie-Division
Division Nr. 408
269. Infanterie-Division

Order of battle (1 Mar 1945)

Festung Glogau
Kampfgruppe 16. Panzer-Division
Panzerkorps "Großdeutschland"
Divisionsstab. 615
21. Panzer-Division (most)
Kampfgruppe Panzer-Grenadier-Division
  "Brandenburg"
Kampfgruppe Fallschirm-Panzer-Division 1
  "Hermann Göring"
Kampfgruppe 20. Panzer-Grenadier-Division
  V. Armeekorps

Kampfgruppe 342. Infanterie-Division
Kampfgruppe 72. Infanterie-Division
275. Infanterie-Division
XXXX. Panzerkorps
Kampfgruppe 25. Panzer-Division
Divisionsstab Matterstock
SS-Brigade "Dirlewanger"
Divisionsstab. 608
35. SS- und Polizei-Grenadier-Division
Brigade.100

Order of battle (12 Apr 1945)

LVII. Panzerkorps
6. Volks-Grenadier-Division
72. Infanterie-Division
Panzerkorps "Großdeutschland"
Panzer-Grenadier-Division "Brandenburg"
Divisionsstab z.b.V. 615
Kampfgruppe 545. Volks-Grenadier-Division
Panzer-Ausbildungs-Verband "Böhmen"
Korpsgruppe General der Artillerie Moser
Division Nr. 193

Division Nr. 404
Division Nr. 463
V. Armeekorps
344. Infanterie-Division
Kampfgruppe 36. Waffen-Grenadier-Division
  der SS
214. Infanterie-Division
275. Infanterie-Division
Kampfgruppe 35. SS- und Polizei-Grenadier-
  Division

Order of battle (30 Apr 1945)

4. Panzerarmee
269. Infanterie-Division
LVII. Panzerkorps
6. Volks-Grenadier-Division
72. Infanterie-Division
17. Infanterie-Division
Gruppe Kohlsdorfen
Divisionsstab. 615
Divisionsstab. 464
Kampfgruppe 545. Volks-Grenadier-Division
Panzerkorps "Großdeutschland"
Fallschirm-Panzer-Division 1 "Hermann
  Göring"
Panzer-Grenadier-Division "Brandenburg"
  20. Panzer-Division
Korpsgruppe General der Artillerie Moser

(subordinated to Panzerkorps
  "Großdeutschland')
Division Nr. 193
Division Nr. 404
Fallschirm-Panzerkorps "Hermann Göring"
Fallschirm-Panzergrenadier-Division 2
  "Hermann Göring"
Kampfgruppe "Frundsberg"
LXXXX. Armeekorps
Division Nr. 464
Division Nr. 469
Division Nr. 404
Kampfkommandant Chemnitz
Stellvertretendes IV. Armeekorps
  (Wehrkreis IV)
Kampfkommandant Dresden

Order of battle (26 Jan 1945)

5. Panzerarmee
167. Volks-Grenadier-Division
3. Panzer-Grenadier-Division
LXVII. Armeekorps
277. Volks-Grenadier-Division
3. Fallschirmjäger-Division
89. Infanterie-Division
246. Volks-Grenadier-Division

XIII. Armeekorps
18. Volks-Grenadier-Division
326. Volks-Grenadier-Division
9. Panzer-Division
LXVI. Armeekorps
560. Volks-Grenadier-Division (remnants)
15. Panzer-Grenadier-Division
26. Volks-Grenadier-Division

Order of battle (1 Mar 1945)

LXXIV. Armeekorps
3. Fallschirmjäger-Division
85. Infanterie-Division
272. Volks-Grenadier-Division
LXVII. Armeekorps

Order of battle (12 Apr 1945)

XII. SS-Armeekorps
363. Infanterie-Division
Stab Oberst Witte
Kampfgruppe 3. Fallschirmjäger-Division
59. Infanterie-Division

Order of battle (21 Jan 1945)

LXVII. Armeekorps
277. Volks-Grenadier-Division
89. Infanterie-Division
3. Fallschirmjäger-Division
XIII. Armeekorps

Order of battle (31 Mar 1945)

6. Panzerarmee
Kampfgruppe 356. Infanterie-Division
I. SS-Panzerkorps
1. SS-Panzer-Division "Leibstandarte SS
    Adolf Hitler"
3. SS-Panzer-Division "Totenkopf"
Kampfgruppe Hungarian 2nd Armoured
    Division

Order of battle (12 Apr 1945)

I. SS-Panzerkorps
Kampfgruppe Keitel
Kampfgruppe 356. Infanterie-Division
1. SS-Panzer-Division "Leibstandarte SS
    Adolf Hitler"
12. SS-Panzer-Division "Hitler Jugend"
Generalkommando Schultz
710. Infanterie-Division

89. Infanterie-Division
277. Volks-Grenadier-Division
Korpsgruppe Botsch
18. Volks-Grenadier-Division
26. Volks-Grenadier-Division
LXVI. Armeekorps
5. Fallschirmjäger-Division

LVIII. Panzerkorps
183. Volks-Grenadier-Division
9. Panzer-Division
12. Volks-Grenadier-Division
353. Infanterie-Division
62. Volks-Grenadier-Division

246. Volks-Grenadier-Division
18. Volks-Grenadier-Division
326. Volks-Grenadier-Division
9. SS-Panzer-Division "Hohenstaufen"

12. SS-Panzer-Division "Hitler Jugend"
232. Panzer-Division
II. SS-Panzerkorps
2. SS-Panzer-Division "Das Reich"
Hungarian 1st Mountain Brigade
6. Panzer-Division
Hungarian 1st Cavalry Division

Kampfgruppe Oberst Staudinger
II. SS-Panzerkorps
Kampfgruppe Oberst Folkmann
Kampfkommandant von Bünau
2. SS-Panzer-Division "Das Reich"
3. SS-Panzer-Division "Totenkopf"
6. Panzer-Division
Führer-Grenadier-Division

Order of battle (30 Apr 1945)

1. SS-Panzer-Division "Leibstandarte SS
Adolf Hitler"
Kampfgruppe 356. Infanterie-Division
12. SS-Panzer-Division "Hitler Jugend"

Generalkommando von Bünau
710. Infanterie-Division
II. SS-Panzerkorps
3. SS-Panzer-Division "Totenkopf"
Führer-Grenadier-Division

The Author

Ian Baxter is a military historian who specializes in German twentieth century military history. He has written more than twenty books including 'Wolf' Hitler's Wartime Headquarters, Poland – The Eighteen Day Victory March, Panzers In North Africa, The Ardennes Offensive, The Western Campaign, The 12th SS Panzer-Division Hitlerjugend, The Waffen-SS on the Western Front, The Waffen-SS on the Eastern Front, The Red Army At Stalingrad, Elite German Forces of World War II, Armoured Warfare, German Tanks of War, Blitzkrieg, Panzer-Divisions At War, Hitler's Panzers, German Armoured Vehicles of World War Two, Last Two Years of the Waffen-SS At War, German Soldier Uniforms and Insignia, German Guns of the Third Reich, Defeat to Retreat: The Last Years of the German Army At War 1943–1945, Biography of Rudolf Hoss, Operation Bagration – the destruction of Army Group Centre, and most recently The Afrika-Korps. He has written over one hundred journals including 'Last days of Hitler, Wolf's Lair, Story of the V1 and V2 rocket programme, Secret Aircraft of World War Two, Rommel At Tobruk, Hitler's War With His Generals, Secret British Plans To Assassinate Hitler, SS At Arnhem, Hitlerjugend, Battle Of Caen 1944, Gebirgsjäger At War, Panzer Crews, Hitlerjugend Guerrillas, Last Battles in the East, Battle of Berlin, and many more. He has also reviewed numerous military studies for publication and supplied thousands of photographs and important documents to various publishers and film Production Company's worldwide.